Clare Crossman (1954–2021) was a much-valued Shoestring poet. Her four collections – *The Shape of Us* (2010), *Vanishing Point* (2013), *The Blue Hour* (2017), and the present collection – appeared at regular four yearly intervals. Each of them is distinguished by its attention to the craft of poetry and, most particularly, by its masterly interpenetration of the natural and human worlds. As Tamar Yosselof perceptively remarked, she is 'interested in the minutiae of things, their colours and moods and shapes.' And Roger Garfitt, in commending her 'poetry of unflinching celebration,' rightly implies that her work reveals an unshowy attentiveness whose virtues speak for themselves. 'Beautiful and unsettling,' Joanne Limburg calls this work, 'not to be missed,' John Greening notes. No, indeed, and, though the poet herself is now prematurely dead, the best of her writing will long survive her.

THE MULBERRY TREE

THE MULBERRY TREE

CLARE CROSSMAN

Printed by imprintdigital
Upton Pyne, Exeter
www.digital.imprint.co.uk

Typesetting and cover design by The Book Typesetters
us@thebooktypesetters.com
07422 598 168
www.thebooktypesetters.com

Published by Shoestring Press
19 Devonshire Avenue, Beeston, Nottingham, NG9 1BS
(0115) 925 1827
www.shoestringpress.co.uk

First published 2021

ISBN 978-1-912524-58-7

ACKNOWLEDGEMENTS

Thank you to the editors of The Lake, The High Window, Pennine Platform, London Grip, Coast to Coast, Atrium Press, Poetry Birmingham, Frogmore Papers, Scintilla, Fourteen, DreamCatcher. Poems for the NHS . Overstep books Barnard, Fragmented Voices, Wildcourt, Ink, Sweat and Tears. Poem of the North. Atrium, As Above so Below, Postcards to Malthusia.

'Another Compass' was commissioned as part of the Lucy Cavendish College Cambridge. Science and Poetry Festival Autumn 2019 and read at the event.

'The Night Toby Denied Climate Change' was selected from open readings for Letters to the Earth. Harper Collins 2019.

Thank you to my friends James Murray White, Bell Sellkie, Helene Hinn, Luke Hughes Davies, Ann Graal, Roger Garfitt, Lucy's Sheerman and Hamilton. Kaddy Benyon and Stav Paula.

The three of us fog up the rainy windows.
Talking, ironing, imagining mulberry acres.
Spun to this unlikely filament.

– White Kimono, Mark Doty

For my brother David, Ursel, Sarah and Iain always.

CONTENTS

1 THE MULBERRY TREE

2 THE TERRITORY OF WATER

3 THE WHISPERING LAND

4 POEMS FOR RIVER GELT, NORTH CUMBRIA

5 THE THICKENING

1 The Mulberry Tree

THE MULBERRY TREE

Nothing was ever wasted: elastic bands,
old envelopes, paper bags put neatly
away. It was because of the war,
that might come back; and so we had to
eat our greens, not leave the crusts on bread
pretend to like rice pudding.

Jam was made from berries of the mulberry tree.
Kept high on shelves in the cool basement,
rusty red, almost amber, sweeter than raspberries.
'The lovers tree' she called it:.
Soft wood, gnarled and leaning,
a garden feature for years.
We were allowed to climb it,
imagined we'd find rolls of silk.
Slept beneath it in a tepee; unafraid.

We had seen the rubble.
The shells of houses with no floors,
the strange murals of fireplaces
imprinted on high walls.
But could not imagine what it was like
if bombs fell out of the sky.

We were the future, held in photographs,
bright against the day.
The lucky ones, swinging on branches
of a golden age; come out of a terrible
knowledge, into a lengthening shade.

A PHOTOGRAPH

Here we are, framed in the rinsed light
of 1950's black and white, sitting
beside my mother on a small chintz sofa.
Three and five, my brother and myself
in our hand-knitted cardigans. His feet
stick out in sandals, I have a grin
and one tooth missing.
My mother always in her best, set hair,
sapphire brooch and pearls. This flat
is where we live. We lean.

In memory, my father is at the other
end, with us in between. Owl glasses,
bald head and serious face.
But in reality he is absent - in his office,
organising, writing letters, answering the phone.
But perhaps it was lunchtime
and he came home to eat a tomato and
horseradish sandwich and take this photograph.

And I think now, that this is what
childhood is: being with the two people
who made you, talking, eating,
sleeping, washing up together.
Until it seems boring,
so the edges fade and curl.
And grown up, you leave easily,
without realising
this is what you have.

KENTISH

These were her phrases:

'I see you thousands didn't!" she'd say
as we scuffed home. One foot in the gutter,
the other on the pavement.
'Who do you think you are, the Duke of Turkey?'

How well she knew that a penny was the difference
between walking and riding. Her one stout pair of shoes,
and housekeeper's coat, hair up in a net.
'Waste not, want not', her mantra.

'Are you likely to be took any worse?'
Her response to noise or the getting of steam for colds.
When she clanked and poured from enamel jug to bowl.

'It was a dark and stormy night, and the rain came down in torrents."
The beginning of her one story:
Told to us in our warm beds until we fell asleep,
Dreaming of the oceans she described.

Night after night, as we grew up,
cared for and cherished.
The wind changed, and we got *stuck like that,*

And on *a lick and a promise,* she was gone.

WALTON STREET

My grandmother would embroider
large pink roses until Captain Russell,
her admirer, in his bowler hat and pinstripe,
came to dinner his gin would fizz
with tonic in a crystal glass,
and he would tell bad jokes, make puns.

Not caring for convention, then
they would dance around
the Irish wooden table
which held the onyx sculpture
of a small child with a bow.

And it did not matter that nothing matched,
their smoke and silver candelabra
guttering shadows as they talked
in a house of wonders.
The mirror's depth held pools
of light like a wide lily pond.
And in the afternoon,
the figures on the London pavements
could be seen walking beyond the lifting nets.
The shift and strangeness of it was part
of a sepia stained evening of uncertain gold.

Upstairs, outside my room
the skyline was a waltz of Chelsea chimneys
and the moon.
Each irregular shaped roof
laddering the city.

JOHN GODBY

We always met John Godby on the walk to school.
Dressed in a too small suit, his hair brylcreamed flat
a neat side parting and a pair of wireframe NHS glasses.

He never spoke. His mother, permed, in a good coat
talked instead. She replied. 'We are fine thank you,'
when Nan asked 'How are you Mrs Godby?'

Then they would move on in perfect step
her shepherding him, looming at his shoulder,
as if he was a sheep or far too clever for the likes of us.

'There is no Mr Godby' we were told. 'He died
in the war.' That woman and that boy, on their own,
seemed quite other to us.

So we made jokes at his expense. About his squint,
the plaster over his eye, his disinfected comb
and how we could tell the time from them.

8.15, no more, no less'. Both impossibly neat,
she propelling him, kept always in plain sight,

in case he too one day was inexplicably lost.

BOY WITH A FISH

You were the boy with a fish
proudly dangling a flat skate, as large
as yourself, on the deck of a Falmouth Trawler.

Then you were a boy who made bowls:
bashed and moulded clay, firing it
to make cavernous shapes.

I spoke for you because, at first,
you were deaf and found words slipped.
We played together in the sand.

Later, saved by careful knowledge,
you chose mending and medicine,
pulling miracles up from the dark, like lobsterpots.

The shape of a life is an arc of time,
it lengthens, shortens, slows, like the nylon reel,
the sudden tug on the line.

Maybe there was never a pattern,
just diving down to discover,
then rising and holding a fine pearl aloft.

Brother and sister, we are the echo
of the years we spent in childhood's rooms.
Now our hair is fading to white

like the tide and the surf. We can't go back
except on this poem's plumb line.

THEATRE GOING

We are sitting at the front balcony, in an unlikely row.
My father's jagged tweed elbows, leather patched,
his legs stuck out. His mother in her fur coat,
marquisate pinned, damp from the rain
and smelling of tobacco: the tickets for this
matinee were expensive, there is no turning back.

In the orchestra pit instruments are tuning up.
Riff of the saxophone scale, slight melody
of violin. Coughing, a breath then a roll of
drums, announcing The Mikado overture.
A triumphant melody:
'If you want to know who we are!'

The curtains open. A story is being sung by
people with ridiculous names: Pish-Tush and Nanky Poo.
Courtyards and kimonos imprinted with
a ceremony of clouds, telling a fairy story:
a prince disguised as a minstrel,
an orphan rescued by a queen.

Afterward, outside a London Street,
the rain drops on our shoulders catch
the counterpointing lamps, the lightest of disguises.
No longer at the edge of it,
we run to the tube, and in the way of luminosity,
the flowers seller has a bucket of
different coloured chrysanthemums,
their rich flounce and elegant petals,
full of all we have to say.

DANDELIONS 1962

At the derelict municipal garden,
we picked bunches from behind
the overgrown band stand.
Laburnum, (oriental lantern flowers),
Lilac (every drifting hem), cherry blossom
(old fashioned) and cow parsley (organza trace).

Some, we pressed under heavy books
to lie between thick pages.
Kept in the dark they lost their colour
their beauty faded to pale and tissue thin,
a list of names.
We wrote by hand in ink:
name, date when found.
Dandelions stained our fingers
and their intangible gossamer clocks
drifted away, moth like.

In winter, we would
conjure the flowers again:
with paints on paper, making a new book
where they rambled in profusion
and were wild. Tumbling and falling
keeping the difference
of their own light and summer;
beyond classification.

GERMANY 1964

He took us travelling every summer
in the clapped-out Zephyr.
Ferry to Ostend and then
delighting on the autobahn,
past Cologne and Frankfurt,
Germany's fast road toward
The Bremmer Pass.
We stopped to feel the texture
of each place we passed through.
Black Forest dark, freezing Austrian lakes,
black bread, sauerkraut and sausages
and then the twisted thread of the Mosel;
its thin towers, hills and distant tiny Schloss.
We made halts for lunch,
breathed in another country, swatted flies.
Slept in plain rooms with heavy dark furniture,
carved wooden wardrobes, feather pillows,
thin curtains and forgettable florid wallpapers,
wooden floors that were scrubbed clean.

For him it was a remembered place
where if there had never been a war
he might have owned a vineyard
and would have been someone entirely different.
The languages he spoke coming back to him,
in his knowledge of the Rhineland architecture
of towns and music.

After the mountain snow the heat of a pitiless blue sky;
he laid out at our feet the possible world,
certain in his conviction that the fast roads
and strange cuisines were the future.
That borders were for crossing,
and windows for opening over courtyards into air.

A FRIENDSHIP

She says she wants to find bohemia,
and so we talk for longer as we saunter down the road.
How to give it definition?
To me her fair hair is golden while I am
short and dark. Maybe I think there is
something inside that connects us:
We seem to understand the tricks that surfaces
play and the importance of far away.

So in our 1970's astrakhan coats we continue
our conversation. We buy vivid patterned
dresses in a hippy style,
decorate our bedsits with bead curtains,
and second-hand books.

Single girls, uncertain of who we are,
we both come from ordinary places where
time is seasons and the movement of the sun.
We have read a lot of novels.

How we translate our narratives
will be the work of years.

WHAT WE KEPT

We carried away those things
we could not bear to leave.
A pair of white iron stone jugs glazed
with blue patterns and a single white rose,
the Bakelite black horse book ends
that supported antique editions.

They had marked our lives at home,
all the coming and going.
In the hall on the days where there was
nothing but sun, always standing in place.

Small legacies of the years and days
we spent together.
They had the years imprinted on them,
a copper lustre.

The ringed hands that touched them,
the voices from the corridors,
and remembered rooms,
an attic, a great grandfather's house
leaving dust.

This is what was known to us.
The shape those objects made on the air.
Of these in that time and place.
We kept their history silently,
while we could remember
who we were and where we belonged.

2 The Territory of Water

All these memories
I take them home with me
The opera, the stolen tea,
The sand drawings, the virgin sea
Old years ago.

– Verdi Cries. June Tabor.

CHALK STREAM LULLABY

'O sisters, let's go down to the river to pray'. – Alison Krauss

I can see why ancient tribes gave
rivers gods: votive statues, carved tokens,
silver coins, bronze rings.

If I bring any gift it's my shadow.
My white feet in the water,
the grass whistle I blew between my hands.

Small offerings made to the clarity of the stream,
to the flow, the glint in the gravel,
as a charm, as a prayer.

When bindweed is threading white dust,
all inscriptions lost, falling and mossed:
a morning of pooled sun beside

the crossing pole for travelling over.
Water boatmen, hover flies,
lift of a moorhen's wing.

A green shimmer after a narrowing
under bent trees. Like a first love,
a small redemption, a psalm of trickling light.

FOR KATE

You are sitting in the back while I am
driving and we are listening to the album
that you loved by Carole Bayer Sager:

'I'd rather leave
while I still believe the meaning of the words.'

It's that day again, when we crossed
the moor to Haworth and rivers flooded
the road, so we could sail downstream.
I remember how the drops fell
on the skylight of the attic in your house.
A savage lullaby
falling on the station cat,
the sensible women with umbrellas:
making a difficult music
of new birth and drownings.
Drumming a rhythm
impossible to live without,
impossible to stay dry and remain.

And so I am writing this for the rain
that never seems to leave the valley.
This note you didn't leave,
this letter you will never read.
About the day we turned for home
when groups of plovers were flocking
on the air, caught in late winter
weather and the new spring wind
into which you chose to go.

BIRD WATCHING

'It's a joy to be hidden, but a disaster not to be found'. – D. W. Winnicott

The walls you painted years ago are
enough for you. White and a Chinese screen
that provides colour. You live plainly
and know that when you look out
of the kitchen window to the roofs
there will be no one at your shoulder.

When you come home, after a day of listening
to other people's stories, everything
is as you left it. The unwashed plate,
the novel you are reading, fraught messages
caught in the answer phone until you listen.

You like alone. The clarity of it
a rhythm punctuating your days.
The walk to the tube for work
and the contemplation of what's
been hidden. Starlings and pigeons
flock above your head.

In high summer you follow them
wagtails, oystercatchers, swallows
on the sweep of Norfolk marshes.
Thinking of those you love and loved,
on the sharp rising of their curves
and tilt of wings.

They define the air as they wish.
Put aside the pavements
the rush, the get and spend.
Defying everything that pins us down.

ANOTHER COMPASS

for Dr Deborah Talmi

From the fire of brain you made maps of memory,
drew patterns of all the feeling places.
Found mind remembered all the ordinary things
but carried different freights.
Some terrible. Some every day.
Knife to a throat, a child starving or
two women drinking coffee at a table.

Like sunlight when it moves through water,
catching particles of dust, each image carried different weights.
There was more than reason, the years encoded
on our minds, alluvial.
Stories had different depths and beginnings, middles, ends.
Sense being made of the anguish of being left,
the first day in a new room.
Keys, which were not black and white
but shifting. Hammered, as the moon, as memory.

I too strive for contours where boundaries dissolve.
Dark into light, feeling, instinct, insight, none.
To make an echo, a scribbled double,
a painted imitation. I remember how to drive
on narrow roads across wide fields to forget.
How a certain voice recalls summer,
a white room and an ease.

Long ago, we realised that wolves hid in the dark
and berries shone in upland places, so we
learned to avoid forests with lamped eyes.
We are not robots responding to the ringing of a bell
or programmed by a digital code.
But, plural, remembering the smallest things,

knowing how to look: We make, remake, unmake
cannot unsee what we have seen.
Always setting another compass, as lighthouses,
or ships on the horizon, prismatic globes,
flickering, flashing, far out across the dark.

STRING

for Iain

In the thin sun of a mild morning,
the windows streaked with winter light,
I picked up the strong twine
dropped from your pocket,
too short for garden use.

There's something about string.
How it leans with the wind,
supporting foxgloves and runner beans
from endless changes in weather.

How it tightens its purpose to keep
collected things neat, but yields to let
what is enclosed slip.

These rooms where we live together
tied by a loose knot, that shifts and stays
hours full of skeins that stop us falling down.

WOODWICK HOUSE, BIRSAY, ORKNEY

Outside the stone house, half a harvest moon
possible to see each star, the spirals
and curves of the galaxies' borrowed light.

The sea booms and wind catches the lintel,
the temperature drops suddenly at night.
All summer I have lived with the season.

Browned to a chestnut's skin, now I wake
in the morning curled to a husk.
The air is edged with the rind of apples.

The dog, all sinew and clown's eyes, circuits me.
He finds a seagull skeleton, the shape of a hare.
On this square of land, a clear brown burn

falls through the garden to the shore
where other islanders travel by boats
to their farms.

Tides pool over stones and shells.
Rain catches the light on an autumn road.
In September, what more can there be?

THE NIGHT TRAIN

In another life I would have
worked on trains.
The flashing corridor of light
as the carriage arrows forward.
At the coast we hit a shower of rain.
It spatters across the halts
beading the dark. In flight,
I imagine the next city, sleep and doze
through the rise and fall
of ringing phones and conversations.
Always moving on belonging nowhere.

At the crossings, headlights are dipped
like artificial moons and on the platform
people disperse into the hollow night
like constellations, white faced,
waiting for the next connection.

Outside the steamed-up window,
all the people it is possible to meet.
At dawn the smudge of cafes
and lit houses over the fields.
Leaving or returning, the wheels
thunder, horizons and new towns.
I wake up in the morning
from a lullaby or a dream,
somewhere else, touched and taken
unable to look back, gone my own way.

KAVAKI (CYCLADES)

Sun inhabits my bones, sand sticks in my hair.
Resin and creak of another country: sea
and mountain dust. Enough to stand in the light.
Scattered geology of islands, archipelago
of sailors and gods. We travel to each port
by water which is turquoise,
cerulean, indigo smudged.

Under the vines old men play cards.
Their wives dressed in black, sit across from them
at a wooden table. The wind
turns the heavy windmill sails
between scattered white churches.
The throw of the dice, the luck of the draw,
the hand you are dealt. What remains is
gesture and argument, everyday inscribed
in the wondering light.

All things fall with their gods. We exist
purely in time. In this thin place, simple
and ancient on the border of spirit
and bone, earth and sky, skin browned
to paper, it would be easier to lift
the shifting veil on the plain stone places.

NOTES ON SUFFOLK

The fields begin with sea-going oaks
close to tiny roads winding through copses which
have no fences and fold trees into arching tunnels,
remote as any mountains. Possible to get lost here
and never be found, in houses hidden down long avenues.

Then there is the question of the sky that blows
like an enormous canvas. From shingle to the Dutch coast,
its own flag of salt and air. The night fisherman's beacons
glimmer at the sea's edge. Everywhere defined by light.

I will not drive you to the place where the plough
hails stones on windscreen, like a passing storm.
But rather if it rains, we will find a junk shop that sells
tea and cake, and is decorated with Staffordshire figures:

a woman's hair pinned up in ringlets,
spaniel at her hems, the man in a blue braided tunic.

And though we know because of circumstance and tides
that this could never have been, why is it that
the marsh, the clinking boats, seem to know us
and take us in?

HOW WE VANISH

It's a year since the damp Sunday
when we were summoned to Ward 2.
You lay between white sheets
with others who were waiting to wake or move,
like solitary sleepers who have forgotten
time. Our vibrant friend who at 78
loved to dance and arrived at our doors with cake;
felled by a stroke. Wired up to machines.
We read to you but all the poems
made us weep for you and for ourselves.
Told you had lost all speech and would not walk again,
we held your hands

And I realised in that absence that this is
how we vanish. Without fanfare.
Behind walls and windows with shut blinds.

TWO LETTERS

1   *Unsent*

I want to tell you as you sit in this one room
that the London Streets you left are just the same.
The city square you loved is inscribed
with green traces and magnolia blossom.
The railings outside the school where you taught
still bounces with children.

The light here floods in from the distant view
and you remember your mother's evening dresses,
your father's terrible jokes and jaunty smile.
This is your come and go: all that happened before.
So I won't say bedridden or house bound but
rather the woman who can laugh when I read
her John Betjeman. Who has lost all time,
and refuses to let it grow shabby in her heart.

2   *Winter Letters*

They were still in their envelopes,
where I put them into dust and dark.
They seemed imprinted with the day
they were written, frank of a postage
stamp, ink blurring an old address.
I thought of you walking down a darkened street.
Posting them, leaving the desk where you wrote.
The heft of our feelings textured in sentences.
They would arrive on frosty cold mornings,
lie on the mat. Only tearing or burning
would delete your ghost shape.
Part of us folded between the pages,
like calligraphy as we talked
across distances in a slow hand.

THE TERRITORY OF WATER

On Neptune Street,
you may be dreaming of how the tide
will take you South to where two seas
meet, halfway to Africa, halfway to Spain.
Along the shore the harbour opens;
black sea shingle and the scudding tide.

One bag on your shoulder
clanking with all you possess
like a sailor, you will come to know the ocean,
the departure, the arrival, the return.

Once boarded for the journey
there is no going back, unless the compass
sets a course for home.
The deck will heave and roll
below the flight of cormorants

above the whispering sea
where storms break mountainous waves,
and calm is flat and stifling,
the sky a lid that can't be lifted.

In the territory of water
the book of maps you opened,
will fill with fireflie's gold ignition.
Sudden changes in weather.
Red burn of sun on sea,
the purple outlines of harbours,
their unknown warmth and scents,
sail bound jetties, beyond grey.

Vermillion dusting your hands,
in black wet October,
turning pages will tell about
the wind you saw.
The glint at each corner
of the constellations,
the tin cup of water lifted, the sky
inking, poems, songs and legends.

3 The Whispering Land

I tell a wanderer's tale,
The same I began long ago, a boy in a barn
I am always lost in it.
The place is always strange to me.

"Encounter at St Martins" – Ken Smith

WEARSIDE PHONE CALL

Sunday, and your voice drops from the satellite,
freighted with vowels, soft like sanded oak's grain.
'Darlo'. Speech well-worn like the cobbles in your road.
'Love, shall you be going to that?'. Travelled language,
easy, open and close, like the back yard gate.
Burr of dialect absorbed different worlds.
Factory and settlement. Migration from hill and salt.
Our conversations clear as a whistle, worn as coins.

I hear the valley when you speak.
See the neat square of daylight in your window.

Then, I am of moorland. Marra. Held firm in the wind's hollow.

marra: friend/mate

THE WHISPERING LAND

Out on the fell in the wind-staunch houses,
someone will come in from the weather,
take off the bluster of their coat, knock mud
from boots inside the fiercely closed door.
The fire lit to claw back warmth from
the wind's boom, vans parked up beside
the hen coop: those who live here have room
above their heads, know the ground below their feet.

There are walks over thrown stepping stones,
grey stone bridges, and valleys to drive through
between lit doors. The old trees fill with leaves
every summer, their shadowy tunnel *omert;*
corridors to walk through unseen.
Until meeting, in the sandstone towns,
streets are greened with conversation
and long dreams
born from the whispering land:
water's rising, marshed fields.

I think of them as the people of the sky,
the fabric of the place turned and spun
from horizons, where to be is enough.

omert: densely covered by trees. Cumbrian dialect

SHOPHILL COTTAGE, KIRKHOUSE, CUMBRIA

We enter upstairs into what once
were the eaves used for the storage of bolts of cloth,
strong cotton, pairs of boots.

Now through the windows, there's a view
of the farm, square with fan windows,
solid with years and a flock of sheep.

It was a peopled place, needing a shop,
a counter to lean on, scratch of a pen,
somewhere to visit for meeting and gossip.

The track by the wall once was a railway
that carried shale from mines for fired
bricks to make houses.

Is this why the house holds us so gently,
finding society in our footsteps,
our shouts between rooms?

The hill wives have left no ghosts
of the years they arrived out of wild weather.
The place left to settle and creak

in a slow rise of dust, miles from anywhere,
no longer an empty house on the road.

OUTRAKE

Gan along the road to tha bad bend
where three lonnins meet at lane end.
That's the start of coo-stripplins hill.
A curd of yellow in wall, below broken byre:
windows slit in stone for the drying of straw.
Wood's a cop of firs to brek wind off moor.

Furst field opens with tup folds, grass and river.
Path teks you up through sandstone quarry
and hikey-dikey walls.

Land belongs to Johnston brothers.
Auld like their collies, they are
not in fine fettle and taken badly.
East are fences, clagg and clart,
you'll drop down six miles over.

Circle back, along beck, where cows
come to drink from the washpool.
Kings Farm is below brickworks yard
where Armstrongs are digging for
shillies again.

It's to these lonnins
wild hares will come when all yats
are broken and corbies
come circling over the stones.
And I mind some of us will ken
wild valleys, fell footpaths,
the straight coffin tracks,
the lang stretch of river's journey.
Across here thirt is always an outrake
as everything rests on the tilt of a star.

Outrake: an extensive open pasture. A path leading to pasture from enclosed fields.

Coo-stripplins: cowslips.

Lonning: track.

Cop: bank of earth on which a hedge grows.

Byre: Barn.

Tup: male sheep or ram.

Hikey-dikey: childrens jumping game.

Clag and clart: mud and bog.

Washpool: swimming place.

Shillies: gravel.

Yats: gates.

HEARTWOOD

At the shallow gravelled beck,
water has grown harebells, fragile
and blue. Beyond the streets and bridges
the roads I walked to work.
Among the sandstone houses,
this is the place that held me
with its low mossed walls,
curve of fells and valleys,
answering back only
in silence and weather.

Under the blackthorn tree, suddenly
I am walking fie-berried snow.
And behind the white blossom
hawthorn hedges, my mother and father
sit opposite each other, talking by the fire.

The hawthorn and the rowan,
giving definition to what might be called
belonging, might be called home
and is a heartwood.
Like a lost map of years ago:
a history written on the land,
caught in the light-filled windows
of white farms and the ripening sloes.

4 Poems for River Gelt, North Cumbria

GREEN SHELTER

Dried leaves in deep woods
just breaking green.
The river surfs red sandstone;
dents and dimples,
has its own hush in
amber water spinning
to a honeyed rush.

A heedless spool
cutting a deep channel,
a long brown thread
speaking in fern tongues,
difficult to catch.

There is much to ask the river.

EARTH PSALTER

Stone-keeper. way-maker.
Palm-shaper. depth-maker.
Honey-spun. crimson dyed.
Path-to-follow. Fish-pooler.

Grief-water. Pain-breaker.
Shade-gatherer.
Storm road, flood maker,
Force-of-nature, bridge breaker.

High tilt. Great force.
Channel cutter.
Quarry-miner.
End-of-days bringer.

Weir rush, shelter-weaver,
Horse-brown-ice. road-skater.
Waterfall. Rain-collector.
Wild charmer.
Long muse.

Earth psalter.

POTHOLES

In the disused quarry cave
Lichen grows, ferns drip rain
here's an echo of somewhere ancient.
Saxophone a voice
would be a tinder struck,
planted, rising, answering back to the land.

The tide of history and the river
is fall and rise, rise and fall.
Here it boils zigzagging, left to right
following the sandstone layers,
cutting limestone platforms
making whirlpools at gravity's gathering point.
A tornado of water twisting, sucking you
in with its music of stones chiselling
potholes in the banks large as cannon balls
is an impossible well.

The path on the bank is washed
to stepping stones by a sudden spring.
Tree roots grasp the air.
Here is the flood, uncontained.

The tide of history is fall and rise,
rise and fall.
The quarry and the cauldron know this
they are reaching for the sea.

IN ASHLYN WOODS

Take some recycled corrugated iron,
lichened covered, from decades of use
some wooden planks to build a wall
and French windows that were
never fitted. Use nails to cobble them
together. Remember an Edward Hopper
painting of the East Coast where storms
have weathered all the homestead beams.

Close to the trees and the wind's book
in the early sun children can swing
on long ropes or laze in hammocks
slung between each trunk.
Under the awning make an open fire
for heat, light, a kettle's smoke and rattle.
Surround the circle of the hearth
with second hand armchairs.

This is a parallel world, an ancient geography,
hay bales and hazel branches frame
in a grain of somewhere other.
Later bees will come and
in the long grass you'll leave your shape,
beside the pond, on the small island,
where you drew breath
among the berries, bird song
and the sky reaching of white nettles
where the woods led you.

SIT PLACES

for Belle

I walk there most mornings
to the green stretching of the fields
and stand leaning in the shade of trees
between two corridors of light.
And I think how the land can own
places with its calligraphy,
how it writes in old tracks
hedges, tussocks
and ragged edges where nobody goes.

When there's a small bridge over thin water.
the ditch runs underneath,
greening with weeds and dragonflies.
Time around me like the river
in deep quiet under the sky.
There are always two horses,
they snuffle and eat the grass.
I envy their long patience,
the wild they know.

But here, where the larks dance,
this ordinary moment is a statement
for another way of being.
Air above my head, ground below my feet.
In a stillness, nothing owned
enough to watch and be.

YGGDRASIL

World tree of deep shade, connecting sky and earth,
the rings told seventy years when it was felled,
nine worlds and summers written in its girth.

Of magic, shadows and the night's gold
decay grew in its trunk which winter weather
rotted out with frost and so the wood was sold.

No shelter from the rain when it is stormy
leaves like stars have fallen a green veil,
branches stacked and burned, becoming history.

Smoke writes on the winter sky, a silver scale.
The stump remains to mark the ash was there
like illustrated pages of a Grimm's fairy tale.

Across the snowed lawn the footprints of a hare,
on the Black Fen there is a shiver,
no legends left or birdsong, the garden fence is bare.

For want of wood we cannot sail a river,
without the heavy branches, no music in a gale.
For want of trees there is no fireside glimmer.

Without the ash the moon has nowhere to sail.

5 The Thickening

For the last blossom is the first blossom
and the first blossom is the last blossom
and when from Eden we take our way
the morning after is the first day.

– Apple Blossom, Louis MacNeice

SOMEBODY CATCH MY BREATH

Is grafittied in red paint under the road bridge
I walk past every morning.
How it describes my sense of falling.

Somebody catch my breath.

I found a thickness of cells, reinventing shape
re-writing who they are in these green days.
The summer is a shadowed tunnel now.

Somebody catch my breath

How bright the hawthorn shines.
If I am leaving now. How will I begin
to become their beautiful light?

DISCUSSING PHILIP LARKIN IN ONCOLOGY

Here in the waiting room queue,
where everyone is trying to do
their best,
someone has brought sandwiches
to soften the wait,
and the hours of chemotherapy
as chemicals drop in.
The conversation turns to,
'not like it in my day!' jokes
to tame time, and the terror of it.

At my appointment you, a concerned
doctor, ask me if I've read Larkin?
And I remember a grainy art house film:
him in bicycle clips and a three quarters mac,
looking through black-rimmed glasses
at the modern age. What would he have made
of counselling? Head massage?
The Macmillan pod?
Something curmudgeonly.

So I agree, it helps to know his poetry here.
Under high windows bleak with sun,
that glance witness to our passing through.
Beyond the clinical corridors, the lateness
and delays, when something's being said,
 it's love and wit survive of us.

We watch from the train,
let the curtains lift,
as the trees leaf, the days exist.
Arriving here, when arrow showers fall as rain.

CHEMISTRY

He said look at it this way, all this is natural,
think of the Adriatic Sea
its warmth and strange red blooms,
perfect sea salt formulation
and crystals.
And then there's yew:
needles collected in mud-soaked lanes
on winter afternoons before cold weather,
taken away in vans for pressing.

That night I dreamt about myself
and my best friend teaching girls to dance
I smelt the orange blossom
the warm rain as if I was in that evening.
I was also holding high branched amulets,
to ward off the evil eye.

And there were other women on the path.
Their names tattooed in blue become
warriors like me too long from home.
The water writing in their bodies
from the ground below their feet.

And it was not a myth that
somewhere miles away in a dense forest
there were biologists examining each root
and tiny flowers for chemistry.

Detailed and botanical as
eco system, slip stream, puja,
protein, vein, liquid, pistil, stamen,
DNA. As Culpepper
when the world slipped.

IN PATIENT

In the afternoon I lie on my back
listening to the voices in the ward.
They seem to sparkle in the light
caught on water's surface, continuing
beyond the place where they have
fallen from the sun.

On the 9th floor propped on the hospital bed
above the long white corridors,
they take me out to where the tide
exists, beyond the coffee rooms, trolleys,
porters, clinics and the heli pads
to where I can float again.

Wordless I am held up; much as by
the earth, salt water or a mild day
of autumn air that is made of footsteps,
laughter and faces looking in.

The reach of hands seems a river,
and the rush of it lifts me above
the floors below, on a clear tunnel
of a rising lighthouse beam.

WARD D9

for Linda and Helen

We are a murmuration of rose-ringed parakeets,
plumed in our floral nightdresses, flashes of colour.

Turning our heads sideways to catch each other's
eye, as we rise and fall on our beds unable to keep still.

The nurses visit us for our inexplicable laughter
and ability to talk. Having taken the swoop,

and arrived here by escape or accidental release,
we are still on the loose: perching,

wisecracking,
from a source not quite understood.

We did not choose this, I and the other
two women who delight in answering back.

Neither victims nor heroines. On this cancer ward
between the sheet changing and the drips,

we remain, flightless, piratical
look down from the windows, shameless

still hoping for air and spreading our wings.
From deep in our feathers we mutter:

Give us a chip! Turned out nice again!

Pieces of eight, pieces of eight.

FEMME FATALE

My hat is crocheted wool,
almost a hair net or snood.
From the shadows of a Bette Davis
film in black and white
I enter rooms flaunting a black butterfly.
Sequined, embellished, like an exotic stranger.

I have joined the shorn and short haired women
who let time show on us and no longer
pretend to understand fashion.
We have experimented with
the postulant or Vermeer girl,
(a simple wimple made of cloth)
or the rose-embroidered turban,
bamboo knit for comfort,
afternoons of ennui, being Blanche du Bois.
We have been shown great kindness.

Like a small sisterhood of Buddhist nuns
in the temples of haberdasher shops.
Full of the wisdom of crochet, velvet
gypsy scarves, and beanies.
See our robes and bells, forget
our missing parts.
We do not need you to pray for us
or be told that in the moment
is where we should live.

Talk to us.

THE NIGHT TOBY DENIED CLIMATE CHANGE

We were sitting like a group of Vervet monkeys
beside a fire in a bucket, casting shadows,
trying to keep warm.
Above us the stars trailed with light
from where they were no longer.
And I remember all the other times
when we had said: How can we stop
the sudden heat? The melting and the floods?
The yearly losses of birds, the lack of cuckoo song,
the hunger and displacement.
In my head I made a list of everything we'd lose,
Cornflower, dock, radish, oak summer,
Earwigs, bees, crows, potatoes, cabbages,
but it was far too long and being animal
I remembered that I could live on berries,
green leaves, roots from underground
grown in a patch of earth.

Then Graham said, 'For goodness sake!
Look at this ring of firelight.
We need to make more fires and circles for the soul,
across the beaches and hills
lanterns for Gaia.
Not just a label, or a clever name
but light and conversations, to bring changes.
See all those others, across the distance.'

And Toby shrugged and grinned and said
'OK I'll carry on'!
(Luckily it was December,
the cold frost time called winter,
that has snow
and it still mattered to hope).

THE SUSPENDED WORLD

I have seen those who knew the war
walking together like Old Testament prophets.
I have seen a lone white-haired man lifting dumb bells.
I have seen in nod and smile a new courtesy
announcing suddenly, we are postulants.

I have heard the wind through the woods
and an early bumblebee that does not care.
And two larks rising over fields
beside the road full of cars going
to the ghost city. The larks reminded me
of those ascending the cliffs of Dover in 1914
Vaughan Williams knew

The dog still wild wades down the river
chasing deer. A lift of heart.

Now there is the quiet of our rooms,
the shadows and the clock
at different times of day.
A life simplified to moving, breathing,
if we can, under the innocent flowering
of the cherry blossom trees.

At night the pillows soft against the dark
are a presence, a scarf of ordinary things.
As for others who have loved and lost,
been ill for a long time, this is a place
beyond the suspended world.
Sunlight outside the window
and memory, like the early speedwell
I saw, tiny, blue, at the pat's edge.